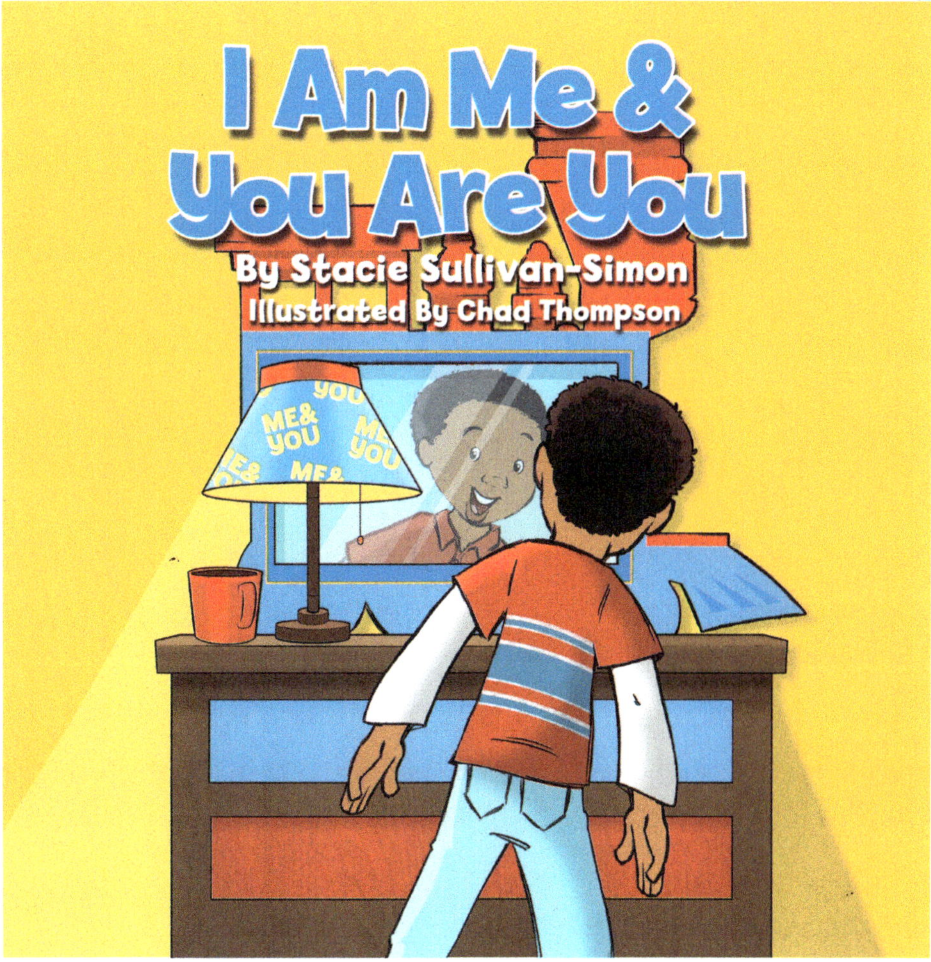
I Am Me &
You Are You
By Stacie Sullivan-Simon
Illustrated By Chad Thompson
ME&
YOU

Halo
Publishing International

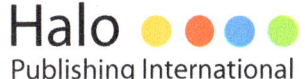

Copyright© 2017 Stacie Sullivan-Simon
Illustrated by Chad Thompson
All rights reserved.

No part of this book may be reproduced in any manner without the written consent of the publisher except for brief excerpts in critical reviews or articles.

ISBN: 978-1-61244-556-4
Library of Congress Control Number: 2017907330

Printed in the United States of America

Published by Halo Publishing International
1100 NW Loop 410
Suite 700 - 176
San Antonio, Texas 78213
Toll Free 1-877-705-9647
www.halopublishing.com
e-mail: contact@halopublishing.com

Dedication

I dedicate this book to my two children Skylar & Mason whom I love very much. Always remember that you are beautiful just as you are, natural curly hair and all. Go forth and be leaders, not followers. Last, but not least, always speak out against injustice!!!

Recent events in the world have inspired me to write a children's book about racism and bullying. Both racism and bullying are learned behaviors that need to be eradicated once and for all!! I can only hope that instilling kindness, understanding, and tolerance in our children at an early age will help them learn that treating others differently based on skin color or disabilities is not acceptable behavior. I can only dream that one day this book will ultimately improve race relations worldwide.

I am me and you are you. Please don't treat me like I'm different than you. When I wake up in the morning, I do the same things as you. I jump out of bed, and put my slippers on too!!

Then I wash my face, brush my teeth, and go potty like you. But I am me, and you are you.

When I look in the mirror, what do I see?
I see my eyes, my ears, my nose, my mouth
and my teeth.

When I look at you, what do I see? I see your eyes, your ears, your nose, your mouth, and your teeth. But you are you, and I am me. When you look at me, what do you see?

My skin color is different, and I may have curlier hair, but don't treat me like I'm different because that's just not fair. Put yourself in my shoes, and think how it would feel if someone treated you differently based on your skin color or hair. It doesn't feel good. And it makes me feel sad.

I may look different, but I am beautiful just like you and that makes me glad.

When you see me at school, let's play and have fun. Let's not focus on things that don't matter, like your skin color or mine, and let's run, run, run!

When you're walking down the street and see me, smile and don't frown.

Take a chance!

We might just become best friends!!!

Always remember, I am me and you are you. We are all beautiful when we let our hearts shine through.

CPSIA information can be obtained
at www.ICGtesting.com
Printed in the USA
BVOW05s0333120617
486550BV00004B/6/P